Visit us at
SequoiaKidsMedia.com
for bonus downloadable content

Written by Todd and Peggy Snow

Photographs © Shutterstock.com: Air Images; ecco; Monkey Business Images; Eric Glenn; rubinat; xuanhuongho; Kassandra Mareeva; Heder Zambrano; Robert Kneschke; Ben Molyneux; Lopolo; besunnytoo; BAZA Production; Prostock-studio; anvinoart; wavebreakmedia; Stephanie Zieber; Brocreative; Rido; TATYANA Yamshanova; MPH Photos; Alim Yakubov; Iakov Filimono; madtom; HowLettery; Cosmic_Design; funbutterfly.

Published by Sequoia Kids Media,
an imprint of Sequoia Publishing & Media, LLC

Sequoia Publishing & Media, LLC,
a division of Phoenix International Publications, Inc.

8501 West Higgins Road, Chicago, Illinois 60631

Customer Service: CS@SequoiaKidsBooks.com

www.SequoiaKidsMedia.com

Library of Congress Control Number: 2022908730

ISBN 979-8-7654-0039-5

Friendliness is a positive way to treat others.
It's shown with kind actions and words.
Like saying nice things and being willing to share.
Friendliness is a way to show you care.

Friendliness is in you to make eye contact. It lets people know you're interested.

Smile and ask...

This is how others are friendly too.

Friendliness is in you to invite kids to join a game. Explain the rules if they need to learn.

FUN FACT:

Babies recognize friendship before they can walk or talk.

Games can be fun when lots of people play.

Include others to make their day!

Friendliness is in you to treat animals kindly. Ask permission before you touch someone's pet.

Extend your hand for them to smell.

Pet gently and speak softly as well.

FUN FACT:
Dogs, horses, elephants, and even whales form lifelong friendships outside their species.

Friendliness is in you to share.

It's polite to offer some of what you have.

If you bake cookies or have a treat, share to be friendly and sweet.

DID YOU KNOW? Sharing ideas and personal feelings is an important part of making friends.

Friendliness is in you to help someone who's sad. Maybe they're lonely or feel left out.

FUN FACT:

"The only way to have a friend is to be one."—Ralph Waldo Emerson

Ask questions to see what's wrong. It can help others to feel they belong.

Friendliness is in you to be happy for others. You can be glad for someone's success.

DID YOU KNOW?

Exchanging a bracelet is a way of showing friendship.

When they do something well,
cheer to let it show.
Or give a compliment
so they'll know.

Friendliness is in you to be respectful.
We're **ALL** equal and deserve the same.

Take turns, be kind, and play fair.
This lets people know you care.

DID YOU KNOW?
National Friendship Day occurs on the first Sunday of every August.

Friendliness is in you to accept differences. People come in all shapes, sizes, and abilities.

FUN FACT:
In East Africa men hold hands as a sign of friendship.

Be yourself—
ask questions to
understand and learn.
Friends will do the
same in return.

Friendliness is in you to help others in need. Collect food and toys to donate.

Giving is a friendly thing to do.
It feels good for them and you.

Friendliness is in you to welcome others. Is there a new kid at school?

Say "Hello." Ask "Where are you from?" Invite them to visit or do something fun.

DID YOU KNOW?
Good friends always try to share and listen to each other.

Friendliness is in you to pay attention.

DID YOU KNOW?
It's normal to sometimes disagree with friends.

Listen when someone talks.

Think about what they say. Nod your head or say "Okay."

Friendliness is in you to show good manners.
"Please" and "Thank you" are the right words to use.

Say "Good morning" and "Goodnight."
Practice your manners to be polite.

You can be friendly in many ways. Think of others and let them know they matter.

FUN FACT:

Research proves that having good friends reduces stress.

Show it each day with what you say and do.

Friendliness is in **YOU!**

FRIENDLINESS BOOSTERS

I will be friendly to all people and animals.

I will be a good friend by listening and paying attention.

I will treat others how I like to be treated.

I will invite others to play and share my toys.

I will make everyone feel welcome and included.

I will greet people with a smile and say "Hello!"